21st
Century
Junior
Library

Flowers

by Jennifer Colby

CHERRY LAKE PUBLISHING * ANN ARBOR, MICHIGAN

Published in the United States of America by Cherry Lake Publishing
Ann Arbor, Michigan
www.cherrylakepublishing.com

Consultants: Elizabeth A. Glynn, Youth Education Coordinator, Matthaei Botanical
Gardens and Nichols Arboretum, University of Michigan; Marla Conn, ReadAbility, Inc.

Photo Credits: © Neirfy/Shutterstock Images, Cover, 6; © Katrina Leigh/Shutterstock Images, 4;
© artpritsadee/Shutterstock Images, 8; © Anna Kucherova/Shutterstock Images, 10; © John L.
Absher/Shutterstock Images, 12; © anuphadit/Shutterstock Images, 14; © Willi Schmitz/Shutterstock
Images, 16; © NKLRDVC/Shutterstock Images, 18; © Kathy Clark/Shutterstock Images, 20

LIBRARY OF CONGRESS CATALOGING-IN-PUBLICATION DATA
Colby, Jennifer, 1971-
  Flowers/by Jennifer Colby. – [Revised edition]
    pages cm.—(21st century junior library)
  Includes bibliographical references and index.
  ISBN 978-1-63188-035-3 (hardcover)—ISBN 978-1-63188-121-3 (pdf)—
ISBN 978-1-63188-078-0 (pbk.)—ISBN 978-1-63188-164-0 (ebook)
  1. Flowers–Juvenile literature. I. Title. II. Series: 21st century junior library.
  SB406.5.C65 2014
  635.9–dc23   2014006278

Cherry Lake Publishing would like to acknowledge the work of
The Partnership for 21st Century Skills.
Please visit www.p21.org for more information.

Printed in the United States of America

CONTENTS

leaves

stem

roots

A plant has many parts.

Plant Parts

Each part of your body has a special job. Your lungs breathe. Your ears hear. All the parts work together to help you live and grow.

Did you know that plants also have parts that work together? Roots take in water from the soil. Stems take that water to the leaves. The leaves use that water to help the plant live and grow.

5

There are many kinds of flowers.

A flower is another part of a plant. Flowers look pretty, but they also have a special job. They make seeds. Each seed can make another plant.

Let's take a closer look at flowers.

Think!

Many people's first names are also the names of flowers. Who do you know that has a flower name?

Do you see the yellow pollen grains on this flower's stamens?

How Seeds Are Made

A flower has many parts. Flowers often have **petals**. In the center of the petals are different parts of the flower. The **stamens** look like threads. The **pistil** has a flat top.

Stamens hold **pollen grains**. A pollen grain can be as small as a speck of dust. Each stamen is covered with many pollen grains.

Apples are a fruit that we can eat. There are many seeds inside an apple.

Pollen grains land on top of the pistil and get stuck. Now the flower is **pollinated**. It can make seeds. Part of the pistil changes after the flower has been pollinated. It grows into a **fruit**.

The growing fruit protects the seed inside of it. Some seeds are smaller than a grain of sand. Other seeds are as large as a soccer ball!

Look!

Find a flower. A tulip works well. Ask an adult before you pick one! Gently pull off the petals. Can you see the pistil, stamens, and pollen?

Hummingbirds are just one kind of animal that helps flowers make seeds.

How do animals help a plant by visiting its flower? A butterfly lands on top of a flower. The butterfly sucks the nectar of the flower through its long **proboscis**. The butterfly knocks against the dusty stamens as it moves around the flower. The butterfly's legs and body become covered with pollen.

Soon the butterfly flies to a different flower. The pollen grains fall off the butterfly. They land on the flower's pistil. Now this flower is pollinated.

Bees and other animals help pollinate flowers.

There are many other animal pollinators. Watch a flower garden on a summer day. You will see insects flying around. Bees, flies, beetles, and butterflies all pollinate flowers.

Birds and other animals can pollinate flowers, too. Hummingbirds love to drink the sweet nectar of a flower. Bats pollinate flowers at night.

Think!

Bats pollinate flowers in deserts. They like pale flowers with strong smells. Pretend you are a bat. What would attract you to pale flowers at night? Did you say "the scent of the flower"? That's right!

Wheat is a plant that people grow for food. It is pollinated by the wind.

Blowing in the Wind

Grasses and trees also have flowers. Sometimes these flowers can be hard to find. Some flowers are very small. Some do not have any scent or petals. These flowers do not attract animals.

These kinds of plants do not need animal pollinators. Wind blows their pollen around. Pollen is blown from the flower of one plant to the flower of the next plant.

The fruit of the maple tree flies in the wind like tiny helicopters.

Many trees are pollinated by the wind. Corn, wheat, and other crops are also pollinated by the wind.

Flowers can be pretty or plain. They might smell good. That is not their only job. A flower's most important job is to make new plants.

Create!

Cut out some flower pictures from old magazines. Cut out some pictures of animal pollinators. Make a collage of flowers and their animal helpers.

GLOSSARY

fruit (FROOT) the part of a plant that holds the seeds

nectar (NEK-ter) juice made by flowers to attract animals

petals (PET-uhlz) parts of a flower that are usually brightly colored

pistil (PIS-tl) the part of a flower where seeds are made

pollen grains (POL-uhn GRAYNZ) dust-size pieces that help make seeds in flowers

pollinated (POL-uh-ney-ted) having had pollen moved to one flower from another

proboscis (proh-BAS-kis) a long, thin tube that forms part of the mouth of some insects

stamens (STAY-mehnz) parts of a flower that make pollen

FIND OUT MORE

BOOKS

Macaulay, Kelley. *What Are Flowers?* New York: Crabtree Publishing Co., 2013.

Whitehouse, Patricia. *Flowers.* Portsmouth, NH: Heinemann, 2009.

WEB SITES

PBS Parents–Activities: Exploring Flowers

www.pbs.org/parents/catinthehat/ activity_exploring_flowers.html
Children and parents can explore flowers with these science crafts, conversation starters, and activities.

StudyJams–Scholastic: Flowers

studyjams.scholastic.com/studyjams/ jams/science/plants/flowers.htm
Watch a fun video describing flowering plants and the process of reproduction.

BBC–Schools Science Clips–Life cycles

www.bbc.co.uk/schools/scienceclips/ ages/9_10/life_cycles.shtml
A virtual laboratory where you can dissect a flower, label it, and put it back together again.

INDEX

ABOUT THE AUTHOR

Jennifer Colby is a school librarian, and she also has a bachelor's degree in Landscape Architecture. By writing these books she has combined her talents for two of her favorite things. She likes to garden and grow her own food. In June she makes strawberry jam for her children to enjoy all year long.